21
Principles

21

Principles

Divine Truths

TO HELP YOU LIVE

BY THE SPIRIT

RICHARD G. SCOTT

DESERET
BOOK

SALT LAKE CITY, UTAH

Library of Congress Cataloging-in-Publication Data

Scott, Richard G., 1928– author.
  21 principles : divine truths to help you live by the spirit / Richard G. Scott.
    pages cm
  Other title: Twenty-one principles
  Includes bibliographical references.
  ISBN 978-1-60907-526-2 (hardbound : alk. paper)
  1. The Church of Jesus Christ of Latter-day Saints—Doctrines. 2. Mormon Church—Doctrines. 3. Holy Spirit. 4. Spiritual life—The Church of Jesus Christ of Latter-day Saints. 5. Christian life. I. Title II. Title: Twenty-one principles.
  BX8656.S365 2013
  248—dc23   2013001376

Printed in the United States of America
Publishers Printing, Salt Lake City, UT

10   9   8   7   6   5   4   3   2   1

Contents

Introduction

Humankind has always benefited from obedience to true principles. The fearless Polynesians in precarious craft crossed an immense ocean for destinations thousands of miles away. That feat was accomplished not by chance but by adherence to sound principles of celestial navigation. They prepared carefully and did not succumb to temptations to deviate from their course or delay en route. In like manner, you and I can be assured of reaching worthy objectives in life by understanding and consistently following correct principles rooted in revealed truth.

Principles are anchors of safety. They are like the steel anchors a mountaineer uses to conquer otherwise impossible cliffs. They will help you have confidence in new and unfamiliar circumstances. They will provide you protection in life's storms of adversity.

Joseph Smith's inspired statement, "I teach them correct principles, and they govern themselves," still applies (quoted by John Taylor, in *Millennial Star,* 15 Nov. 1851, 339). The Lord uses that pattern with us. You will find correct principles in the teachings of the Savior, His prophets, and the scriptures—especially the Book of Mormon. While easy to find, true principles are not easy to live until they become an established pattern of life. They will require you to dislodge false ideas. They can cause you wrenching battles within the secret chambers of your heart and decisive encounters to overcome temptation, peer pressure, and the false allure of the "easy way out." Yet, as you resolutely follow correct principles, you will forge strength of character available to you in times of urgent need. Your consistent adherence to principle overcomes the alluring yet false lifestyles that surround you. Your faithful compliance to correct principles may generate criticism and ridicule from others, yet the results are so eternally worthwhile that they warrant your every sacrifice.

As you seek spiritual knowledge, search for principles. Principles are concentrated truth, packaged for application to a wide variety of circumstances. A true principle makes decisions clear even under the most confusing and challenging circumstances. It is worth great effort to organize the truth we gather to simple statements of principle. I have tried to do that with gaining spiritual knowledge. The result is now shared in hope that it will be a beginning place for your study.

21 Principles

1. The Savior's injunction to "ask, and ye shall receive; knock, and it shall be opened unto you" (3 Nephi 27:29) is a gate to spiritual guidance. I learned that gentle promptings will encourage us to make the right decisions. When carefully observed, these gentle impressions to our heart can be followed by specific counsel given to our mind. That counsel leads us to know what to do with greater precision.

2. The scriptures teach, and I have been led to confirm, that we will never be prompted by the Holy Ghost to do something we cannot do. It may require extraordinary effort and much time, patience, prayer, and obedience, but we can do it.

3. Repeatedly I have been impressed to learn that to reach a goal never before attained, one must do things never before done.

4. I have learned that our mind can strengthen an impression of the Holy Ghost or sadly, can totally destroy it by

casting it out as something unimportant or the product of our own imagination.

5. I have been taught that we can make many choices in life, but we cannot choose our final destiny. Our actions do that.

6. When facing adversity, we can be led to ask many questions. Some of them serve a useful purpose; others do not. It really does no good to ask questions that reflect opposition to the will of God. Accepting His will, even when it is not fully understood, brings great peace and, over time, understanding.

7. I have been led through personal experience to understand an important truth: I know Satan has absolutely no power to force a determined, righteous individual because the Lord protects that person from him. Satan can tempt; he can threaten; he can attempt to appear to have such power; but he does not possess it.

8. It is sometimes very hard to discern an answer to prayer for a matter for which we have very deep personal feelings or something which causes strong emotions to arise within us. That is why it is important to receive valid, inspired counsel when one finds himself or herself in such a circumstance.

9. On occasion the Lord will give us vital spiritual guidance by inspiring others to share what they have learned. Such mentors can greatly enrich our lives through thoughtful communication of their knowledge and experience.

10. I have been taught by the Holy Spirit, and by observing others, that concepts like faith, prayer, love, and humility hold no great significance and produce no miracles until they become a living part of the individual through his or her own experience, aided by the sweet promptings of the Spirit.

11. Adversity is a part of life. We will all have it because we need it for growth and for the forging of our righteous character. I have learned that the Lord has a consummate capacity to judge our intent. He is concerned about what we are becoming by the choices we make. He has an individual plan for each of us.

12. When I contemplate the access to the limitless power granted by the Lord to worthy men through the priesthood, I am in awe of His extraordinary kindness. I marvel that He is so benevolent as to grant mere men such a supernal blessing.

13. I know what it is to love a daughter of God who with grace and devotion served with the full feminine

splendor of her righteous womanhood. Father in Heaven well knows women are the compassionate, self-sacrificing, loving power that binds together the human family.

14. A happy marriage results from making correct choices prayerfully together. It can transform a house into a place of heaven on earth.

15. The Spirit has taught me that Satan doesn't have to tempt us to do bad things—he can accomplish much of his objective by distracting us with many acceptable things, thus keeping us from accomplishing the essential ones.

16. One of the most memorable and powerful patterns of communication by the Spirit is through dreams. I have learned that when the transition from being fully asleep to being fully awake is almost imperceptible, it is a signal that the Lord has taught something very important through a dream.

17. Sincere love has the potential to exercise power far beyond our limited understanding of love.

18. Satan's temptations are as a two-edged sword—we can be overcome by them or we can resist and gain strength until we can declare, "Get thee behind me, Satan."

19. In a quiet moment of pondering, I learned that there is a relationship between faith and character. The greater our faith in Jesus Christ, the stronger our character, and increased character enhances our ability to exercise even greater faith.

20. Forced obedience yields no enduring fruit. That is why both our Father in Heaven and the Savior are willing to entreat, to prompt, to encourage, and to patiently wait for us to recognize precious spiritual guidance from Them.

21. It is important not to judge ourselves by what we think we know of our own potential. We should trust the Lord and what He can do with our dedicated heart and willing mind (see D&C 64:34).

Principle 1

The Savior's injunction to "ask, and ye shall receive; knock, and it shall be opened unto you" (3 Nephi 27:29) is a gate to spiritual guidance. I learned that gentle promptings will encourage us to make the right decisions. When carefully observed, these gentle impressions to our heart can be followed by specific counsel given to our mind. That counsel leads us to know what to do with greater precision.

COMMUNICATION WITH our Father in Heaven is not a trivial matter. It is a sacred privilege. It is based upon eternal, unchanging principles. We receive help from our Father in Heaven in response to our faith, obedience, and the proper use of agency.

One of the great lessons that each of us needs to learn is to ask. Why does the Lord want us to pray to Him and to ask? Because that is how revelation is received.

When I am faced with a very difficult matter, this is how I try to understand what to do. I fast. I pray to find and understand scriptures that will be helpful. That process is cyclical. I start reading a passage of scripture; I ponder what the verse means and pray for inspiration. I then ponder and pray to know if I have captured all the Lord wants me to do. Often more impressions come with increased understanding of doctrine. I have found that pattern to be a good way to learn from the scriptures.

There are some practical principles that enhance revelation. First, yielding to emotions such as anger or hurt or defensiveness will drive away the Holy Ghost. Those emotions must be overcome, or our chance for receiving revelation is slight.

Another principle is to be cautious with humor. Loud, inappropriate laughter will offend the Spirit. A good sense of humor helps revelation; loud laughter does not. A sense of humor is an escape valve for the pressures of life.

Another enemy to revelation comes from exaggeration or loudness in what is stated. Careful, quiet speech will favor the receipt of revelation.

On the other side of the equation, spiritual communication can be enhanced by good health practices. Exercise, reasonable amounts of sleep, and good eating habits increase our capacity to receive and understand revelation. We will live for our appointed life span. However, we can improve both the quality of our service and our well-being by making careful, appropriate choices.

For spirituality to grow stronger and more available, it must be planted in a righteous environment. It is important that our daily activities do not distract us from listening to the Spirit. Haughtiness, pride, and conceit are like stony ground that will never produce spiritual fruit.

Humility is a fertile soil where spirituality grows and produces the fruit of inspiration to know what to do. It gives access to divine power to accomplish what must be done. An individual motivated by a desire for praise or recognition will not qualify to be taught by the Spirit. An individual who is arrogant or who lets his or her emotions influence decisions will not be powerfully led by the Spirit.

The Lord has declared: "And ye are to be taught from on high. Sanctify yourselves and ye shall be endowed with power, that ye may give even as I have spoken" (Doctrine and Covenants 43:16). The words *sanctify yourselves* may appear puzzling. President Harold B. Lee once explained that you can replace those words with the phrase "keep my commandments" (*Teachings of*

Presidents of the Church: Harold B. Lee [2000], 34). Read that way, the counsel may seem clearer.

One must be ever mentally and physically clean and have purity of intent so that the Lord can inspire. One who is obedient to His commandments is trusted of the Lord. That individual has access to His inspiration to know what to do and, as needed, the divine power to do it.

Detailed direction comes when we readily respond to the initial promptings of the Spirit. At times such spiritual guidance can indicate or imply events that will occur later in life. Our acceptance of such promptings and our willingness to obey do not mean that the will of the Lord will be changed. They do mean that the impact on our life will be different. There will be far more significant consequence because of our willingness to obey the counsel given by such sacred guidance of the Holy Spirit.

When we are acting as instruments in behalf of others, we are more easily inspired than when we think only of ourselves. In the process of helping others, the Lord can piggyback directions for our own benefit.

Our Heavenly Father did not put us on earth to fail but to succeed gloriously. It may seem paradoxical, but that is why recognizing answers to prayer can sometimes be very difficult. Sometimes we unwisely try to face life by depending on our own experience and capacity. It is much wiser for us to seek through prayer and divine inspiration to know what to do. Our obedience assures that, when required, we can qualify for divine power to accomplish an inspired objective.

Principle 2

The scriptures teach, and I have been led to confirm, that we will never be prompted by the Holy Ghost to do something we cannot do. It may require extraordinary effort and much time, patience, prayer, and obedience, but we can do it.

A s you exercise faith in Jesus Christ and in His teachings, you will grow in your testimony of His limitless power to accomplish what He has promised. The key words are *exercise faith*. True faith has enormous power, but there are principles that must be followed to unleash that power. Moroni taught, "Faith is things which are hoped for and not seen; wherefore, dispute not because ye see not, for ye receive no witness until after the trial of your faith" (Ether 12:6; emphasis added). That means you must practice the truth or principle you have faith in. As you live it consistently, there will come a witness of its truthfulness through the power of the Holy Ghost. It is often a feeling of peace. It could be a stirring within you. It might be evidenced by opening doors to other truths. As you patiently look for a confirmation, it will come. Recognize that the Lord will give you the capacity to understand and prove through personal experience the truthfulness of His teachings. He will confirm the certainty that His laws will produce the promised results when obeyed willingly and consistently.

I have often pondered the tremendous accomplishments of the Prophet Joseph Smith. Why was Joseph Smith able to do that which was beyond his personal capacity? It was because of his powerful testimony. That led to his obedience, his faith in the Master, and his unwavering determination to do His will. I testify that as your testimony grows in strength, when needed and earned, you can enjoy inspiration to know what to do and, when necessary, divine power or capacity to accomplish it. Joseph Smith perfected his ability to follow the guidance of the Lord by practiced personal discipline. He did not let his own desires, convenience, or the persuasions of men interfere with that compliance. Follow his example.

Surely our Savior Jesus Christ provides the clearest demonstration of what it means to carry out the Father's will when it seems impossible. I try to imagine what an intensely poignant moment it must have been for our Father in Heaven when the Savior cried out from the cross, "My God, my God, why hast thou forsaken me?" (Matthew 27:46; Mark 15:34). Father in Heaven did not forsake His Son on the cross. The Savior's cry was motivated when He felt removed the sustaining support He had always enjoyed from His Father. His Father recognized that the Savior needed to accomplish the Atonement totally and completely on His own, without external support. The Father did not abandon His Son. He made it possible for His perfect Son to win the eternal fruits of the Atonement.

There is an imperative need for each of us to strengthen our understanding of the significance of the Atonement of Jesus Christ so that it will become an unshakable foundation upon which to build our lives. As the world becomes more devoid of foundational standards and as honor, virtue, and purity are increasingly cast aside in the pursuit of appetite, our understanding of and faith in the Atonement of Jesus Christ will provide strength and capacity needed for a successful life. It will also bring confidence in times of trial and peace in moments of turmoil.

You may sometimes find it difficult to have faith in your capacity to do good in a world that is increasingly evil. But God has provided a way to live in this world and not be contaminated by the degrading pressures evil agents spread throughout it. You can live a virtuous, productive, righteous life by following the plan of protection created by your Father in Heaven: His plan of happiness. It is contained in the scriptures and in the inspired declarations of His prophets. He clothed your intelligence with spirit and made it possible for you to enjoy the wonder of a physical body. When you use that body in the way He has decreed, you will grow in strength and capacity, avoid transgression, and be abundantly blessed.

One Christmas Eve many years ago, in the light of a full moon, I climbed a small hill in the isolated village of Quiriza, Bolivia. Four young elders and I had spent the day crossing over a mountain pass on a treacherous road. Then we struggled up a riverbed to see if the teachings of the Savior would help a destitute people. What we saw that day was discouraging—undernourished children, adults subsisting on meager crops, some with eyes glazed from seeking refuge with alcohol and drugs. I looked at the tiny, barren village below: a cluster of adobe thatched-roof houses beaten by the harsh environment. The only evidence of life was barking dogs searching for food. There was no electricity, telephone, running water, roads, proper sanitation, nor doctors there. It seemed so hopeless. Yet a solemn prayer confirmed that we should be there. We found a humble people who embraced the restored gospel with determination to live it. They did that under harsh conditions where severe poverty, alcohol, drugs, witchcraft, and immorality were in plentiful supply.

Under the guidance of exceptional missionaries, the people learned to work hard to cultivate the fields. They produced a harvest of nutritious vegetables and raised rabbits for better protein. But the best lessons came from beloved missionaries who taught them of a God who loved them, of a Savior who gave His life that they might succeed. Their physical appearance began to change. The light of truth radiated from their happy faces. As devoted, loving emissaries of the Lord, missionaries patiently taught truth to a willing people. Wives and husbands learned how to live in harmony, teach truth to their children, pray, and sense guidance of the Spirit.

I watched a six-year-old boy who had carefully observed our first baptismal service act out with his younger sister what he had seen. He carefully arranged her hands, raised his tiny arm to the square, mumbled words, gently lowered her into a depression in the sun-baked earth, led her to a rock where he "confirmed" her, then shook her hand. The youth learned most quickly. They became obedient to the light of truth taught by the missionaries and in time by their own parents. Through their faith and obedience, I have seen how in one generation youth baptized in that village have overcome a seemingly hopeless future. Some have been missionaries, graduated from universities, and been sealed in the temple. Through their diligence and obedience, they have found purpose and success in life despite an early harsh physical and evil-saturated environment. If it can be done in Quiriza, Bolivia, it can be done anywhere.

That you can accomplish good far beyond what seems possible to your mortal understanding is a certainty. However, your conviction of that reality must come from your own understanding of truth, from your own application of divine law and your willingness to seek the confirming witness of the Spirit. Your testimony may begin from acknowledgment that the teachings of the Lord seem reasonable. But it must grow by practicing those laws. Then your own experience will attest to their validity and yield the results promised. That confirmation will not all come at once. A strong testimony comes line upon line, precept upon precept. It requires faith, time, consistent obedience, and a willingness to sacrifice.

As the mighty eagle, you can rise to glorious heights. You can discover truths that will ignite your spirit. As you combine positive experiences of life with eternal doctrinal truths, you will discover what it means to be a divine child of a Father in Heaven who is perfect. As you apply His truths, they will generate vision in your mind and commitment in your heart. You will be inspired and can have power beyond your own capacity. You can qualify through that divine power to be instruments in the hands of God to accomplish what you could not do alone.

Principle 3

Repeatedly I have been impressed to learn that to reach a goal never before attained, one must do things never before done.

ALTHOUGH THE PRINCIPLE of doing new things to achieve new results applies in many areas of life, the underlying quality is the same. It is creativity. Creativity is what allows us to see things in a new way. We can enhance our ability to think creatively by engaging in pursuits that are different from our normal activities.

Several years ago my wife, Jeanene, asked me to go with her to visit one of her close friends. That friend's husband happened to be a commercial artist. I was fascinated with his ability to use brushes, watercolor, and paper to create beauty. Something inside of me said, "Try it," but my more rational self responded, "You've never had any artistic ability; all you will do is prove that you can't paint anything." Fortunately the feeling to want to try persisted.

I got a few books on watercolor from the library, bought an inexpensive set of paints and a brush, and looked for an isolated place where I could safely try my hand at art without embarrassment. With a sheet of ordinary paper I tried to paint a tree, then other objects. The results, even viewed charitably, were not very good, but I still remember the excitement I felt from doing something I had never done before.

The initial feeling of accomplishment encouraged me to read more and try harder. Later I was privileged to take five lessons from a master watercolorist and teacher, Elliott O'Hare. That experience changed everything. I began to appreciate that much can be accomplished with an understanding of basic principles. I discovered the importance of quality materials. Objective criticism from a knowledgeable friend became an appreciated source of growth. There followed other small but important seeds of reinforcement: a prize at the state fair for a modest painting of sailboats in the fog, and the first sale of a watercolor of a small boy and girl with a fishing rod and dog. Even now, many years later, these experiences bring great personal satisfaction.

It doesn't concern me that I will never be an accomplished watercolorist. Even infrequent efforts to try to express feelings with a brush and paint continue to provide a constantly renewing source of pleasure and benefit. There is an awareness of the miracle of color, subtle transitions in value, dramatic contrasts, and appealing shapes and patterns. Every face is a fascinating study of light and shadow, texture, and hue that speaks volumes regarding character and personality. Eyes have become for me the fingerprint of the soul. Moreover the masterful work of gifted artists has become a refreshing source of inspiration and learning. Most important, I feel that perhaps I am more sensitive to the limitless creative genius of our Heavenly Father and His Beloved Son.

Wherever I go I see beauty in ways that would not have been perceived with the same intensity and variety had I not followed that prompting to try something I had never tried before. I still have that first painting. When I look at it my mind is filled with sweet memories of much that happened in that time of my life, and the satisfaction I have received from modest personal efforts to be creative in many different areas of life.

Search for feelings that prompt you to try something new yourself, and if they are not there strive to generate them. Try art, poetry, prose, music, dance, photography, clothing design, or anything you haven't done before. Otherwise you may never know the thrill of personal creativity nor enter the doors it opens to insight, enjoyment, and wonder.

Every individual has creative capacity. The satisfaction and growth creativity generates is intended for each of us, not just for the most gifted. To try takes courage. A famous watercolorist, Edgar A. Whitney, said: "No door is closed to a stubborn scholar." The most challenging barrier one must overcome is to begin; from there it gets easier and more exciting. Then as you try, realize that you personally are going to be hardest on yourself just when you need the most reassurance. Let your self-evaluation be a source of discovery rather than of destructive self-criticism. Believe in yourself. Doubt destroys creativity, while faith strengthens it.

As your ability increases, you will seek the objective criticism of others more experienced. Find ways to learn basic principles about your field of interest. Enjoy the process of discovery, not just the end result of your efforts. As you experiment with new things you will discover a great deal about yourself that likely won't be revealed any other way.

Try it, and you may open up a lifetime of joy and rewarding accomplishment.

Principle 4

I have learned that our mind can strengthen an impression of the Holy Ghost or sadly, can totally destroy it by casting it out as something unimportant or the product of our own imagination.

FATHER IN HEAVEN KNEW that you would face challenges and be required to make some decisions that would be beyond your own ability to decide correctly. In His plan of happiness, He included a provision for you to receive help with such challenges and decisions during your mortal life. That assistance will come to you through the Holy Ghost as spiritual guidance. It is a power, beyond your own capability, that a loving Heavenly Father wants you to use consistently for your success, peace, and happiness.

What can you do to enhance your capacity to be led to correct decisions in your life? What are the principles upon which spiritual communication depends? What are the potential barriers to such communication that you need to avoid?

I am convinced that there is no simple formula or technique that would immediately allow you to master the ability to be guided by the voice of the Spirit. Our Father expects you to learn how to obtain that divine help by exercising faith in Him and His Holy Son, Jesus Christ. Were you to receive inspired guidance just for the asking, you would become weak and ever more dependent on Them. They know that essential personal growth will come as you struggle to learn how to be led by the Spirit.

What may appear initially to be a daunting task will be much easier to manage over time as you consistently strive to recognize and follow feelings prompted by the Spirit. Your confidence in the direction you receive from the Holy Ghost will also become stronger. I witness that as you gain experience and success in being guided by the Spirit, your confidence in the impressions you feel can become more certain than your dependence on what you see or hear.

Spirituality yields two fruits. The first is inspiration to know what to do. The second is power, or the capacity to do it. These two capacities come together. That's why Nephi could say, "I will go and do the things which the Lord hath commanded, for I know that the Lord giveth no commandments unto the children of men, save he shall prepare a way for them that they may accomplish the thing which he commandeth them." (1 Nephi 3:7). He knew the spiritual laws upon which inspiration and power are based. Yes, God answers prayer and gives us spiritual direction when we live obediently and exercise the required faith in Him.

Now I share an experience that taught me a way to gain spiritual guidance. One Sunday I attended the priesthood meeting of a Spanish branch in Mexico City. I vividly recall how a humble Mexican priesthood leader struggled to communicate the truths of the gospel in his lesson material. I noted the intense desire he had to share those principles he strongly valued with his quorum members. He recognized that they were of great worth to the brethren present. In his manner, there was an evidence of a pure love of the Savior and love of those he taught.

His sincerity, purity of intent, and love permitted a spiritual strength to envelop the room. I was deeply touched. Then I began to receive personal impressions as an extension of the principles taught by that humble instructor. They were personal and related to my assignments in the area. They came in answer to my prolonged, prayerful efforts to be guided in my assignment.

As each impression came, I carefully wrote it down. In the process, I was given precious truths that I greatly needed in order to be a more effective servant of the Lord. The details of the communication are sacred and, like a patriarchal blessing, were for my individual benefit. I was given specific directions, instructions, and conditioned promises that have beneficially altered the course of my life.

Subsequently, I visited the Sunday School class in our ward, where a very well-educated teacher presented his lesson. That experience was in striking contrast to the one enjoyed in the priesthood meeting. It seemed to me that the instructor had purposely chosen obscure references and unusual examples to illustrate the principles of the lesson. I had the distinct impression that this instructor was using the teaching opportunity to impress the class with his vast store of knowledge. At any rate, he certainly did not seem as intent on communicating principles as had the humble priesthood leader.

In that environment, strong impressions began to flow to me again. I wrote them down. The message included specific counsel on how to become more effective as an instrument in the hands of the Lord. I received such an outpouring of impressions that were so personal that I felt it was not appropriate to record them in the midst of a Sunday School class. I sought a more private location, where I continued to record as faithfully as possible the feelings that flooded into my mind and heart. After each powerful impression was captured in words, I pondered the feelings I had received to determine if I had accurately expressed them in writing. As a result, I made a few minor changes to what had been written. Then I studied the meaning and application in my own life of the impressions.

Subsequently I prayed, reviewing with the Lord what I thought I had been taught by the Spirit. When a feeling of peace came, I thanked Him for the guidance given. I was then impressed to ask, "Was there yet more to be given?" I received further impressions, and the process of writing down the impressions, pondering, and praying for confirmation was repeated. Again I was prompted to ask, "Is there more I should know?" And there was. When that last, most sacred experience was concluded, I had received some of the most precious, specific, personal direction one could hope to obtain in this life. Had I not responded to the first impressions and recorded them, I would not have received the last, most precious guidance.

What I have described is not an isolated experience. It embodies several true principles regarding communication from the Lord to His children here on earth. I believe that you can leave the most precious, personal direction of the Spirit unheard because you do not respond to, record, and apply the first promptings that come to you. When spiritual guidance comes, it is well to remember this comment of the Prophet Joseph Smith, "God judges men according to the use they make of the light which He gives them." (*Teachings of Presidents of the Church: Joseph Smith* [2007], 405).

Have patience as you are perfecting your ability to be led by the Spirit. By careful practice, through the application of correct principles, and by being sensitive to the feelings that come, you will gain spiritual guidance. I bear witness that the Lord, through the Holy Ghost, can speak to your mind and heart. Sometimes the impressions are just general feelings. Sometimes the direction comes so clearly and so unmistakably that it can be written down like spiritual dictation by the Spirit (see D&C 8:2).

I bear solemn witness that as you pray with all the fervor of your soul with humility and gratitude, you can learn to be consistently guided by the Holy Spirit in all aspects of your life. I have confirmed the truthfulness of that principle repeatedly in the crucible of my own life. I testify that you can personally learn to master the principles of being guided by the Spirit. That way, the Savior can guide you to resolve challenges of life and enjoy great peace and happiness.

Principle 5

I have been taught that we can make many choices in life, but we cannot choose our final destiny. Our actions do that.

IT CAN APPEAR THAT WE CONTROL outcomes in our life, but we do not. Worthiness, righteousness, faith in Jesus Christ, and the plan of our Father assure a pleasant, productive future, while lying, cheating, and violating the laws of personal purity assure a life of misery here on earth and beyond the veil, unless there is the requisite repentance.

You may be tired of others trying to run your life—always telling you what to do. After all, you have the right to make your own choices. That is correct. You have that right. It is your agency. The secret to solve problems in your life will be found in understanding and using the eternally beneficial interaction of your *agency* and His *truth*.

When others give you advice, have you ever said, "I just don't believe the way you do. Those are your standards and your principles. I have my own"? Please understand that no one can change truth. Rationalization, overpowering self-interest, all of the arguments of men, anger, or self-will cannot change truth. Satan knows that, so he tries to create an atmosphere where one unwittingly begins to feel that he can not only choose what to do, but can determine what is right to do. Satan strives to persuade us to live outside truth by rationalizing our actions as *the right of choice.*

But our Eternal Father defined truth and established what is right and wrong before the creation of this earth. He also fixed the consequences of obedience and disobedience to those truths.

He defended our right to choose our path in life so that we would grow, develop, and be happy, but *we do not have the right to choose the consequences of our acts.* Those who willfully, consistently disobey His commandments will inevitably learn that truth. Our agency does allow us to choose among alternate paths, but then we are bound to the consequence God has decreed for our choices.

Our Heavenly Father gave us truths, some as statements of cause and effect. We call them commandments. They guide our life to happiness. He knew that Satan would try to persuade some to live without fixed standards in life so that decisions would be based on whims, what appears convenient, or what provides the greatest personal return in that moment. In this way, Satan removes the power of truth from one's life so he can take that soul captive.

The painful consequences of sin were purposely put in His plan of happiness by a compassionate Father in Heaven so that you need not follow that tragic path in life. A sinner will not only suffer in this life, but sins that have not been forgiven through true repentance will cause anguish beyond the veil (see D&C 19:4, 15–24).

By contrast, with the gift of the Holy Ghost comes the ability to develop a powerfully sensitive capacity to make the right choices. As you enhance your capacity to sense the direction of that infallible influence, you will avoid disappointment, discouragement, and even tragedy.

The Lord has placed currents of divine influence in your life that will lead you along the individual plan He would have you fulfill here on earth. Seek through the Spirit to identify that path and carefully follow that direction that the Lord has put in your life. Align yourself with it. Choose, willingly, to exercise your agency to follow it. Do not be overcome by concentrating solely on today, its challenges, difficulties, and opportunities. Such preoccupations must not totally capture your attention so as to consume your life. Oh, how I would encourage you to weave deeply into the fabric of your soul the recognition that your life now is a part of a much bigger plan the Lord has for you. You lived part of it in the premortal existence. You were valiant there and came here because you wanted to grow and enjoy greater happiness. What you decide to do now in mortality will affect how well you fulfill that divine, personal plan He has for you.

I do not fully understand how it is done, but this divine current does not take away your moral agency. You can make the decisions you choose to make. Should your choices be wrong, there is a path back—repentance. When its conditions are fully met, the Atonement of the Savior provides a release from the demands of justice for the errors made.

It is wondrously simple and so incomparably beautiful. As you continue to live righteously, you will always know what to do. Sometimes the discovery of that may require significant effort and trust on your part. Yet you will recognize what to do as you meet the conditions for such divine guidance in your life: obedience to the commandments of the Lord, trust in His plan, and the avoidance of anything that is contrary to it. The more closely you conform your life to the doctrine of the Lord, the more capacity you will have to do what the Spirit inspires you to do.

Principle 6

When facing adversity, we can be led to ask many questions. Some of them serve a useful purpose; others do not. It really does no good to ask questions that reflect opposition to the will of God. Accepting His will, even when it is not fully understood, brings great peace and, over time, understanding.

I T IS SO HARD WHEN SINCERE PRAYER about something we desire very much is not answered the way we want. It is especially difficult when the Lord answers *no* to that which is worthy and would give us great joy and happiness. Whether it be overcoming illness or loneliness, recovery of a wayward child, coping with a handicap, or seeking continuing life for a dear one who is slipping away, it seems so reasonable and so consistent with our happiness to have a favorable answer. It is hard to understand why our exercise of deep and sincere faith from an obedient life does not bring the desired result.

At such times, to ask, "Why does this have to happen to me?" "Why do I have to suffer this, now?" "What have I done to cause this?" will lead you into blind alleys. Rather ask, "What am I to do?" "What am I to learn from this experience?" "What am I to change?" "Whom am I to help?" "How can I remember my many blessings in times of trial?"

Willing sacrifice of deeply held personal desires in favor of the will of God is very hard to do. Yet, when you pray with real conviction, "Please let me know Thy will" and "May Thy will be done," you are in the strongest position to receive the maximum help from your loving Father.

This life is an experience in profound trust—trust in Jesus Christ, trust in His teachings, trust in our capacity as led by the Holy Spirit to obey those teachings for happiness now and for a purposeful, supremely happy eternal existence. To trust means to obey willingly without knowing the end from the beginning (see Proverbs 3:5–7). To produce fruit, your trust in the Lord must be more powerful and enduring than your confidence in your own personal feelings and experience.

To exercise faith is to trust that the Lord knows what He is doing with you and that He can accomplish it for your eternal good even though you cannot understand how He can possibly do it. We are like infants in our understanding of eternal matters and their impact on us here in mortality. Yet at times we act as if we knew it all. When you pass through trials for His purposes, as you trust Him and exercise faith in Him, He will help you.

How grateful I am personally that our Savior taught we should conclude our most urgent, deeply felt prayers, when we ask for that which is of utmost importance to us, with "Thy will be done" (Matthew 26:42). Your willingness to accept the will of the Father will not change what in His wisdom He has chosen to do. However, it will certainly change the effect of those decisions on you personally. That evidence of the proper exercise of agency allows His decisions to produce far greater blessings in your life. I have found that because of our Father's desire for us to grow, He may give us gentle, almost imperceptible promptings that, if we are willing to accept without complaint, He will enlarge to become a very clear indication of His will. This enlightenment comes because of our faith and our willingness to do what He asks even though we would desire something else.

Our Father in Heaven has invited you to express your needs,

hopes, and desires unto Him. That should not be done in a spirit of negotiation, but rather as a willingness to obey His will no matter what direction that takes. His invitation, "Ask, and ye shall receive" (3 Nephi 27:29) does not assure that you will get what you *want*. It does guarantee that, if worthy, you will get what you *need*, as judged by a Father that loves you perfectly, who wants your eternal happiness even more than you do.

To recognize the hand of the Lord in your life and to accept His will without complaint does not immediately eliminate the struggles that will come for your growth. But I witness that it is the best way there is for you to find strength and understanding. It will free you from the dead ends of your own reasoning. It will allow your life to become a productive, meaningful experience, when otherwise you may not know how to go on (see D&C 24:8).

The Lord's plan is to exalt you to live with Him and be greatly blessed. The rate at which you qualify is generally set by your capacity to mature, to grow, to love, and to give of yourself. He is preparing you to become as He is. You cannot understand fully what that means, yet, He knows. As you trust Him, seek and follow His will, you will receive blessings that your finite mind cannot understand here on earth.

Principle 7

I have been led through personal experience to understand an important truth: I know Satan has absolutely no power to force a determined, righteous individual because the Lord protects that person from him. Satan can tempt; he can threaten; he can attempt to appear to have such power; but he does not possess it.

MUCH OF THE WORLD is being engulfed in a rising river of degenerate filth, with the abandonment of virtue, righteousness, personal integrity, traditional marriage, and family life. Sodom and Gomorrah was the epitome of unholy life in the Old Testament. It was isolated then; now that condition is spread over the world. Satan tries to skillfully manipulate the power of all types of media and communication. His success has greatly increased the extent and availability of such degrading and destructive influences worldwide. In the past some effort was required to seek out such evil. Now it saturates significant portions of virtually every corner of the world. We cannot dry up the mounting river of evil influences, for they result from the exercise of moral agency divinely granted by our Father. But we can and must, with clarity, warn of the consequences of getting close to its enticing, destructive current.

Satan's increasing influence in the world is allowed to provide an atmosphere in which to prove ourselves. While he causes havoc today, Satan's final destiny was fixed by Jesus Christ through His Atonement and Resurrection. The devil will not triumph.

Even now, he must operate within bounds set by the Lord. He cannot take away any blessing that has been earned. He cannot alter character that has been woven from righteous decisions. He has no power to destroy the eternal bonds forged in a holy temple between a husband, wife, and children. He cannot quench true faith. He cannot take away your testimony. Yes, these things can be lost by succumbing to his temptations. But he has no power in and of himself to destroy them.

The devil has great influence in this world by leading individuals to make the wrong choices. He is the father of lies. Nothing he tempts you to do will have a beneficial outcome—absolutely nothing. The hook may be baited by seemingly attractive promises and outcomes, but he is the master of deceit and his agents are powerfully effective in his cause.

Have you noticed how Satan works to capture the mind and emotions with flashing images, blaring music, and the stimulation of every physical sense to excess? He diligently strives to fill life with action, entertainment, and stimulation so that one cannot ponder the consequences of his tempting invitations. Think of it. Some are tempted to violate the most basic commandments of God because of seductive actions portrayed as acceptable. They are made to seem attractive, even desirable. There seems to be no serious consequence, rather apparent lasting joy and happiness. But recognize that those performances are controlled by scripts and actors. The outcome of decisions made is likewise manipulated to be whatever the producer wants. A recurring pattern of deceit prevails.

One who follows this pattern of deceit tries to appear to have influence and capabilities that He does not possess. Satan is the epitome of this model of life. The adversary is a consummate bluffer. He is extraordinarily able to make people think he has power that he doesn't have. I say that on the basis of personal knowledge. I have been in areas of the world where he has exceptional influence among the people, and I know that a determined person, one who is living righteously and can call on the power of the Lord to help, can avoid any encounters with that evil one. That requires righteous living, it requires faith in the power of Jesus Christ, but it can be done. I know positively that is true. If he had power over our agency, he would have used it long ago. That ought to give you a lot of courage.

Never forget that Satan is a real personage with devoted, capable assistants. They are determined to overpower you, not with an onslaught of serious temptations suddenly presented, but by carefully placed, alluring, seemingly unimportant infractions of your long-established standards. The adversary would use these temptations to skillfully lead you away from the path of righteousness. "Thus the devil cheateth their souls, and leadeth them away carefully down to hell" (2 Nephi 28:21). He knows that as long as you can be led by the Holy Spirit, you can resist him. The Lord has made it possible for you to resist Satan's temptations. When obedient, you will be inspired to know what to do and have the capacity to do it.

Avoid worldly wickedness. Know that God is in control. In time, Satan will completely fail and be punished for his perverse evil. Keep in your mind and heart the truth that God's eternal purpose is for you to be successful in this mortal life. No matter how wicked the world becomes, you can earn that blessing.

Principle 8

It is sometimes very hard to discern an answer to prayer for a matter for which we have very deep personal feelings or something which causes strong emotions to arise within us. That is why it is important to seek valid, inspired counsel when one finds himself or herself in such a circumstance.

PRAYER IS A SUPERNAL GIFT of our Father in Heaven to every soul. Think of it: the absolute Supreme Being, the most all-knowing, all-seeing, all-powerful personage, encourages you and me, as insignificant as we are, to converse with Him as our Father. It matters not our circumstance, be we humble or arrogant, poor or rich, free or enslaved, learned or ignorant, loved or forsaken, we can address Him. We need no appointment. Our supplication can be brief or can occupy all the time needed. It can be an extended expression of love and gratitude or an urgent plea for help. He has created numberless cosmos and populated them with worlds, yet you and I can talk with Him personally, and He will ever answer.

I wonder if we can ever really fathom the immense power of prayer until we encounter an overpowering, urgent problem and realize that we are powerless to resolve it. Then we will turn to our Father in humble recognition of our total dependence on Him.

However, an individual who lets his or her emotions influence decisions cannot be powerfully led by the Spirit. The inspiring influence of the Holy Spirit can be overcome or masked by strong emotions, such as anger, hate, passion, fear, or pride. When such influences are present, it is like trying to savor the delicate flavor of a grape while eating a jalapeño pepper. Both flavors are present, but one completely overpowers the other. In like manner, strong emotions overcome the delicate promptings of the Holy Spirit.

The wise counsel often given to patriarchs to keep their homes and lives free from discord or tension certainly applies to us. Joseph Smith learned that lesson and had the courage to record it for our benefit. Spiritual direction will not come when the spirit is offended by unresolved differences with our loved ones even though they are small. It certainly cannot come in an environment where there is even occasional uncontrolled emotion, disharmony, or anger.

When one is caught in a whirlpool of emotion, it is difficult to find a way out alone. When answers to urgent prayer don't seem to come, it can be that we don't understand some truths about prayer, or because we don't recognize answers when they come. From time to time, we may need additional help to see answers clearly, particularly when our challenges are difficult.

I remember visiting with a young woman who was struggling with a decision she had to make. As we discussed her situation, I said, "You have been a sister missionary. Have you prayed earnestly about this issue?"

"Why? Is there something wrong?" she said.

I said, "It just seems like a logical thing to do. You've learned how to be guided by the Spirit. Why don't you pray about it?" She admitted that she had not done so in the way she had learned on her mission, and agreed that she would try.

The very negative response she got to her prayers led her to a decision that saved her from what clearly would have been a disastrous situation. But, partly because this was a very emotional decision, she needed a little assistance from an outside source to be reminded of how to find the guidance she sought.

Once I had an experience that caused me immense anxiety. It had nothing to do with disobedience or transgression but with a vitally important human relationship. For some time I poured my heart out in urgent prayer. Yet try as I might, I could find no solution, no settling of the powerful stirring within me. I pled for help from that Eternal Father I have come to know and trust completely. I could see no path that would provide the calm that is my blessing generally to enjoy. Sleep overcame me. When I awoke, I was totally at peace. Again I knelt in solemn prayer and asked, "Lord, how is it done?" In my heart, I knew the answer was His love and His concern for me. Such is the power of sincere prayer to a compassionate Father.

Know that our Father in Heaven will always hear your prayers and will invariably answer them. However, His answers will seldom come while you are on your knees praying, even when you may plead for an immediate response. Rather, He will prompt you in quiet moments when the Spirit can most effectively touch your mind and heart. As you seek His counsel in moments of pondering, you will rejoice to find solutions to even your most perplexing problems.

Principle 9

On occasion the Lord will give us vital spiritual guidance by inspiring others to share what they have learned. Such mentors can greatly enrich our lives through thoughtful communication of their knowledge and experience.

ONE OF THE GREAT SOURCES of help we can receive as we make our way through mortality comes from the presence in our lives of mentors, people who want to help us, who are interested in our well-being, who may have had greater experience than we have. Such a person need not be older than we are, but should be someone who is willing to give counsel that is founded in principle and doctrine.

Some of the greatest lessons I have learned in my life have been taught to me by those brethren and sisters who have mentored me, given me counsel, seen me struggling with an issue and taken the time to share their experience and provide tremendous encouragement.

Let me share with you an example of that. President Spencer W. Kimball was a very powerful mentor in my life. On one occasion I was really struggling with something and he taught me a lesson with an example. He said, "What would happen if I put a rotten apple in a barrel of good apples?" Well, I am not a horticulture expert, but I knew the answer that they would go rotten. He said, "What should you do?"

I said, "Turn the barrel upside down, dump it out, and put more apples in it."

He said, "Would that work?"

I said, "Sure."

He said, "No."

Why wouldn't it work? What was I missing? He taught me that you've got to get down in there and clean that barrel out, get rid of all of the rot. Then you can put good apples in and they will stay secure. What was he teaching me? How to live life. When you make a mistake, you want to correct it, clean it out, so that the barrel is full of good apples.

To serve and to intentionally reach out to help each other is a great blessing. When you can become a mentor for another because of personal experience you have gained, do it. Age does not matter; experience does. It is very feasible for an experienced youth to be a mentor to someone very much his or her senior.

Sometimes just the way a person lives provides a mentoring experience for others. Such a mentor in my life was President Ezra Taft Benson. When he was Secretary of Agriculture, he didn't lay down all the principles he had lived with. He built them into what he was doing. My father happened to be on his immediate staff, so I had an opportunity to see a little closer than normal what occurred. Organizations from around the country would organize caravans, hundreds of buses coming into the nation's capital, to pressure him to change his policy. He just stood there, listened to them, and politely said, "No."

They threatened, "We'll have the people vote against you."

"Fine. As long as I have this assignment, this is the way it is going to be."

When I would hear that Secretary Benson was going to be testifying on the hill, I would go up and watch in those committee meeting rooms how this great servant of the Lord reacted under tremendous pressure. He was accused of many things falsely in those hearings, but it never seemed to bother him. His integrity to what he felt was right was so firm and his convictions so deep that he wouldn't let adversity or even false accusation bother him. The only emotion I ever saw in him during these experiences was once in a while the back of his neck would get just a little bit red. That was all. He wasn't movable. He stayed right on the path.

He was one day readjusting and reorganizing those who worked immediately for him, and he called a man into his office and asked him if he would accept the responsibility of being in charge of credit services for the Department of Agriculture. This man had another assignment, a lesser one, in the department, and he said, "Mr. Secretary, I'm very honored and pleased that you would give me that assignment. I really enjoy what I'm doing, and I think I would just like to return to my office." Elder Benson again invited him for this assignment, and he again graciously declined. Finally, Elder Benson said, "Ken, if you have anything in your office you would like, get it, because I would like you to come down here now and serve with me."

That example was a tremendous one for the man who accepted the new assignment. He had an opportunity of living close to a man who was gifted and talented and was also obedient to the teachings of the Lord and was willing to give and share. The example changed his life, and he became a member of the Church. President Benson confirmed him a member. That man was my father. How grateful our family will ever be for the influence of that significant mentor in his life!

Principle 10

I have been taught by the Holy Spirit, and by observing others, that concepts like faith, prayer, love, and humility hold no great significance and produce no miracles until they become a living part of the individual through his or her own experience, aided by the sweet promptings of the Spirit.

I N EARLY LIFE I FOUND that I could learn gospel teachings intellectually and, through the power of reason and analysis, recognize that they were of significant value. But their enormous power and ability to stretch me beyond the limits of my imagination and capacity did not become reality until patient, consistent practice allowed the Holy Spirit to distill and expand their meaning in my mind and heart. I found that while I was sincerely serving others, God forged my personal character. He engendered a growing capacity to recognize the direction of the Spirit. The genius of the gospel plan is that by doing those things the Lord counsels us to do, we are given every understanding and every capacity necessary to provide peace and rich fulfillment in this life. Likewise, we gain the preparation necessary for eternal happiness in the presence of the Lord.

A testimony is fortified by spiritual impressions that confirm the validity of a teaching, of a righteous act. Often such guidance is accompanied by powerful emotions that bring tears to the eyes and make it difficult to speak. But a testimony is not emotion. It is the very essence of character woven from threads born of countless correct decisions. These choices are made with trusting faith in things that are believed and, at least initially, are not seen. A strong testimony gives peace, comfort, and assurance. It generates the conviction that as the teachings of the Savior are consistently obeyed, life will be beautiful, the future will be secure, and there will be capacity to overcome the challenges that cross our path. A testimony grows from understanding truth distilled from prayer and the pondering of scriptural doctrine. It is nurtured by living those truths with faith anchored in the secure confidence that the promised results will be obtained.

I am reminded of an experience that occurred on a nuclear submarine some years ago. A nuclear submarine is different from a regular submarine in the sense that it has an extraordinary power plant, and those who laid the foundation for the development of those power plants did it in such a secure way that, unlike normal craft, a nuclear sub has the ability to go at its highest speed, called flank speed, without any difficulty.

If you get on a normal submarine—a diesel boat—and it is up at nearly flank speed, everybody is on watch, wondering what is going to get carried away first and what is going to break down. Not so in a nuclear plant because they are so carefully designed. It takes hours to build a standard ship up to full power, but in a nuclear plant, as fast as the helmsman can turn the throttle, the plant follows and gives greater compulsion.

On one occasion during the shakedown trials—the time when a submarine is put through all of its paces to make sure that it has been built according to specifications before it is delivered to the navy—a nuclear submarine was at full submergence status going at flank speed as the most critical test of acceptance trials. Everyone knew that if they went very much deeper, the pressure of the ocean on the outside of the hull would collapse the bow and the crew aboard would be lost.

The helmsman noted that there was a slight upturn on the submarine, so he tilted the planes downward to correct that. The submarine started to become level. At that time, there was a power breakdown, so the submarine continued at flank speed going deeper and deeper, and there wasn't any way to change the pattern of the planes. Panic, understandably, broke out among the crew members because they knew that in very few seconds their lives would be taken by the water rushing through the crushed bow. There was, however, a petty officer in the engine room pulling himself along the floor. He reached into a cabinet and turned a switch, activating an alternative power supply that saved everyone's life.

Later on, during an investigation of the incident, the petty officer was asked, "How did you know what to do?" Can you imagine him pulling the manual out and starting to read? He said, "I don't know, I just did it." As they questioned him further, he said, "No, I know why I did it. We went to prototype school, and we went through these exercises that trained us how to react when an emergency came. It was so much a part of me that I didn't realize that it came from training."

That is how to live successfully in this world today. Learn how to live the commandments when there is no pressure on you. Develop the standards and obedience by making correct choices repeatedly and you will develop the character that will sustain you when pressures from Satan come into your life. The principles of the gospel will have become such a part of who you are that they will produce miracles.

Principle 11

Adversity is a part of life. We will all have it because we need it for growth and for the forging of our righteous character. I have learned that the Lord has a consummate capacity to judge our intent. He is concerned about what we are becoming by the choices we make. He has an individual plan for each of us.

ALTHOUGH IT MAY NOT BE a welcome insight, the truth is that you will grow more rapidly through challenge and trial than from a life of ease and serenity with no disturbing elements. The intent of your Father in Heaven is to lift you from where you are to where He knows you will have eternal purpose and unspeakable happiness. By using the talents, abilities, and latent capacities you developed in the premortal existence, He will lead you through growth experiences here on earth. When faced squarely and lived fully without complaint, they will raise you to glorious heights of accomplishment and service. To do all of that during the brief period you are on earth is a tremendous challenge. To accelerate your growth and attainment in his plan for you, sometimes He employs a pattern described on the label of some medicines: "Shake well before using."

Such shaking comes through stirring challenges and stretching tests. You likely have encountered some already. You undoubtedly will encounter others. They may come in the form of an accident, the conferral of a great responsibility, or a move that dramatically changes your surroundings and circle of trusted friends. You may begin educational or professional pursuits that prove far more demanding than anticipated. Perhaps personal illness, handicaps, or the death of a loved one puts seeming barriers in your path. In truth they are more likely giant steps intended to lift you to higher levels of understanding and accomplishment.

How these challenges are confronted is critically important to your happiness and personal growth now and forever.

No one wants adversity. Trials, disappointments, sadness, and heartache come to us from two basically different sources. Those who transgress the laws of God will always have those challenges. The other reason for adversity is to accomplish the Lord's own purposes in our life that we may receive the refinement that comes from testing. It is vitally important for each of us to identify from which of these two sources come our trials and challenges, for the corrective action is very different.

If you are suffering the disheartening effects of transgression, please recognize that the only path to permanent relief from sadness is sincere repentance with a broken heart and a contrite spirit. Realize your full dependence upon the Lord and your need to align your life with His teachings. There is really no other way to get lasting healing and peace. Postponing humble repentance will delay or prevent your receiving relief. Admit to yourself your mistakes and seek help now. Your bishop is a friend with keys of authority to help you find peace of mind and contentment. The way will be opened for you to have strength to repent and be forgiven.

But there is a second source of adversity: the testing that a wise Heavenly Father determines is needed even when you are living a worthy, righteous life and are obedient to His commandments. Just when all seems to be going right, challenges often come in multiple doses applied simultaneously. When those trials are not consequences of your disobedience, they are evidence that the Lord feels you are prepared to grow more (see Proverbs 3:11–12). He therefore gives you experiences that stimulate growth, understanding, and compassion which polish you for your everlasting benefit. To get you from where you are to where He wants you to be requires a lot of stretching, and that generally entails discomfort and pain.

Often we have difficulty mastering lessons the Lord wants us to learn when things are going too well in our lives. When there is suffering and pain, pondering and prayer will help us understand what we are to learn from the challenges we are asked to overcome.

We see such a limited part of the eternal plan He has fashioned for each one of us. Trust Him, even when in eternal perspective it temporarily hurts very much. The path you are to walk through life may be very different from others. He may ask you to do things which are powerfully against your will. Exercise faith and say, Let Thy will be done. Such experiences, honorably met, prepare you and condition you for yet greater blessings. As your Father, His purpose is your eternal happiness, your continuing development, your increasing capacity. His desire is to share with you all that He has.

Have patience when you are asked to wait when you want immediate action. If all matters were immediately resolved at your first petition, you could not grow. You may not always know why your Father in Heaven does what He does, but you can know that He is perfectly just and perfectly merciful. He would have you suffer no consequence, face no challenge, endure no burden that is superfluous to your good. He would not require you to experience a moment more of difficulty than is absolutely needed for your personal benefit or for that of those you love.

True enduring happiness with the accompanying strength, courage, and capacity to overcome the most challenging difficulties comes from a life centered in Jesus Christ. Obedience to His teachings provides a sure foundation upon which to build. That takes effort. There is no guarantee of overnight results, but there is absolute assurance that, in the Lord's time, solutions will come, peace will prevail, and emptiness will be filled.

Help from the Lord generally comes in increments. He can immediately cure serious illnesses or disabilities or even allow the dead to be raised. But the general pattern is that improvement comes in sequential steps. That plan gives us an opportunity to discover what the Lord expects us to learn. It requires our patience to recognize His timetable. It provides growth from our efforts and trust in Him and the opportunity to express gratitude for the help given.

I testify that when the Lord closes one important door in your life, He shows His continuing love and compassion by opening many other compensating doors through your exercise of faith. He will place in your path packets of spiritual sunlight to brighten your way. They often come after the trial has been the greatest, as evidence of the compassion and love of an all-knowing Father. They point the way to greater happiness and more understanding, and they strengthen your determination to accept and be obedient to His will.

Don't let the workings of adversity totally absorb your life. Try to understand what you can. Act where you are able; then let the matter rest with the Lord for a period while you give to others in worthy ways before you take on appropriate concern again.

Some years ago, I was impressed to write a note in the margin of my scriptures next to this verse: "Be patient in afflictions, for thou shalt have many; but endure them, for, lo, I am with thee, even unto the end of thy days" (D&C 24:8). The note reads: "This scripture will have increasing importance in your life in the future. You will come to understand how absolutely true it is." I now realize that it is not the affliction part of that scripture that is important. It is the promise, "I am with thee, even unto the end of thy days."

Please learn that as you wrestle with a challenge and feel sadness because of it, you can simultaneously have peace and rejoicing. Yes, pain, disappointment, frustration, and anguish can be temporary scenes played out on the stage of life. Behind them there can be a background of peace and the positive assurance that a loving Father will keep His promises. You can qualify for those promises by a determination to accept His will, by understanding the plan of happiness, by receiving all of the ordinances, and by keeping the covenants made to assure their fulfillment.

Principle 12

When I contemplate the access to the limitless power granted by the Lord to worthy men through the priesthood, I am in awe of His extraordinary kindness. I marvel that He is so benevolent as to grant mere men such a supernal blessing.

I WONDER HOW MANY MEN seriously ponder the inestimable value of holding the Aaronic and Melchizedek Priesthoods. When we consider how few men who have lived on earth have received the priesthood and how Jesus Christ has empowered those individuals to act in His name, we should feel deeply humble and profoundly grateful for the priesthood we hold.

The priesthood is the authority to act in the name of God. That authority is essential to the fulfillment of His work on earth. The priesthood we hold is a delegated portion of the eternal authority of God. As we are true and faithful, our ordination to the priesthood will be eternal.

However, the conferring of authority alone does not of itself bestow the power of the office. The extent to which we can exercise the power of the priesthood depends upon personal worthiness, faith in the Lord Jesus Christ, and obedience to His commandments. When supported by a secure foundation of gospel knowledge, our capacity to worthily use the priesthood is greatly enhanced.

The perfect role model for use of the holy priesthood is our Savior, Jesus Christ. He ministered with love, compassion, and charity. His life was a matchless example of humility and power. The greatest blessings from the use of the priesthood flow from humble service to others without thought of self. By following His example as a faithful, obedient priesthood bearer, we can access great power. When required, we can exercise the power of healing, of blessing, of consoling, and of counseling, as the quiet promptings of the Spirit are faithfully followed.

One way the Lord helps us is through priesthood blessings. When a worthy priesthood bearer is led to pronounce specific blessings, we can be greatly comforted. Yet there is no guarantee of outcome without effort on our part. Appropriate use of priesthood authority opens a channel of help where the outcome is consistent with the will of the Lord. The blessing resolves those things which are beyond our own capacity to influence either personally or with the help of others. Yet we must do our part for the blessing to be realized. We must strive to be worthy and to exercise the requisite faith to do what we are able. Where it is intended that others help, we must use that help also. It is through the combination of our doing what is within our power to accomplish and the power of the Lord that the blessing is realized.

Once I was awakened by a call from an anxious mother. Her premature child was not expected to survive the night. She asked for a priesthood blessing. As I approached the suffering child, the mother stopped me, looked into my eyes, and asked, "Are you worthy to bless my child?" That was an appropriate question. One never feels completely worthy, but we must do our best to be so. There came a strong prompting to bless the child to recover. The worthy mother continued professional treatment and exercised her faith. The Lord responded with the additional blessing needed. And the child recovered.

It is a sobering responsibility for those who bear the

priesthood to act as agents of the Lord to help those in need. That trust requires faith, worthiness, and a sensitivity to the promptings of the Spirit to communicate the will of the Lord. Also, it is a sobering responsibility for those who receive a blessing to exercise faith, to express gratitude for every degree of improvement observed, and to do all within their power to resolve the need.

Often the real value of something is not recognized until it is taken from us. To illustrate, consider a man who had lost the use of the priesthood through transgression. Later it was returned to him as part of the restoration of ordinances he obtained through full repentance. After the restoration, I turned to his wife and said, "Would you like a blessing?" She enthusiastically responded. Then I looked at the husband, now capable of using his priesthood, and said, "Would you like to give your wife a blessing?" Words cannot express the profound emotion of such an experience and the bonds of love, trust, and gratitude it created. You shouldn't have to lose your priesthood to appreciate it more fully.

I ask you brethren to ponder your personal worthiness to use the sacred authority you hold. I also ask you to consider how consistently you use your priesthood to bless others. You have been blessed to have received the teachings of the Savior, our Lord and Master, Jesus Christ. You worthy men who hold the priesthood have a sacred responsibility to honor that gift from God. You have the blessing to use the authority to act in the name of God to bless the lives of others who depend upon you.

Principle 13

I know what it is to love a daughter of God who with grace and devotion served with the full feminine splendor of her righteous womanhood. Father in Heaven well knows women are the compassionate, self-sacrificing, loving power that binds together the human family.

W HEN I WAS A YOUNG MAN, my father was not a member of the Church and my mother, although she was a wonderful, good woman, was less active. That changed later in our lives, and Mother and Father spent much of their lives as servants in the temple in Washington, D.C. But during my growing-up years I didn't know what it was to have a patriarch in my home or a mother who would teach all of the things an active Latter-day Saint mother can teach her children.

As I was about ready to graduate from the university, I fell in love with a beautiful girl, Jeanene Watkins. It took me a long time to date her. There were a lot of other young men who recognized her qualities. When I was with her it just seemed like time flew by; we had so much fun and she was such a strong, wonderful woman. I could tell she began to have some deep feelings for me also. One night when we were talking about the future she said, "When I marry, it will be to a returned missionary in the temple." I hadn't thought much about a mission at that point or really understood what temple marriage meant. But I went home and couldn't think of anything else. I was awake all night long. I couldn't think of anything in the university the next day. Soon I was at the bishop's office having prayed about the importance of a mission.

Jeanene and I both went on missions, and when we returned we were sealed in the temple. I don't know how I could ever thank her for putting her principles before the feelings of her heart. If you ever doubt the power of a righteous woman to influence a man to good works, remember that story.

So many of our sisters are disheartened, even discouraged, and disillusioned. Others are in serious trouble because of the choices they make. Satan has unleashed a seductive campaign to undermine the sanctity of womanhood, to deceive the daughters of God and divert them from their divine destiny. He well knows women are the compassionate, self-sacrificing, loving power that binds together the human family. He would focus their interests solely on their physical attributes and rob them of their exalting roles as wives and mothers. He has convinced many of the lie that they are third-class citizens in the kingdom of God.

If there is any woman reading these words who wonders about how valuable you are, would you remember that you are the last created, you are the best. He saved womanhood for the final magnificent creation, and you are not to feel otherwise. We need to help those women around us recognize how precious they are.

The daughters of Father in Heaven are extraordinary. Women are different from men in more than physical ways. Women just naturally want to help others, whether they are mothers or not. They have joy in serving others. But we as men must understand they need to know from us whether their nurturing is appreciated and beneficial. I think many women worry about that. So whether you are a husband or a son or a priesthood leader, tell the women in your life specific things that you appreciate in what they are doing so they can know that you are aware of it, and you are grateful for their nurturing that is a part of their divine nature. You may even wish to put it in writing.

I learned from my wife the importance of exchanging notes. Early in our marriage I would open my scriptures to give a talk and I would look down and see a note slipped in the pages. Sometimes they were so tender that I could hardly continue to talk. These precious notes from a loving wife!

I began to do the same with her, not realizing how much she truly appreciated them. I remember one day, I took those little round circles that come when you punch holes to put a paper into a three-ring binder and I wrote on a hundred of them the numbers 1 to 100. I turned them over, wrote her a message one word at a time, scooped the circles up, and put them in an envelope. I thought she would laugh.

When she passed away, as I was going through her private things, I found that she had carefully pasted every one of those circles onto a piece of paper so she could enjoy the message again and again. And she not only kept other notes I had written to her, she encased them in plastic as though they were some kind of a treasure. There is only one note that she didn't put in a three-ring binder, by the way. And it is still in our kitchen. I took the glass off the clock in that room and put a little note in there that says, "Jeanene, it is time to tell you I love you." That is still there and reminds me of that wonderful daughter of Father in Heaven.

When Jeanene was ill, I tried to find supporting scriptures

that would help her. I printed them out and put them around the house. I found each one of those in plastic, carefully protected.

I am sharing these personal things in hopes that men who hear of them will do some of the same. If in your mind you are saying to yourself, "Well, I just don't do those things; she knows I love her and I don't have to say it." Yes, you do! Change and do it and you will find that it will bring both of you great happiness.

Father in Heaven loves and appreciates those daughters who are willing to lay their lives on the altar to bring forth life and to nurture. I am sure that as men we can never appreciate the bonding that comes as a mother carries a child for those nine months.

As mothers, you can detect the individual needs of each child and provide ways to satisfy them. Your divinely given instincts help sense a child's special talents and unique capacities so that you can nurture and strengthen them. Consider these examples of how compassionate love and sensitivity of parents, particularly mothers, bless children's lives:

A mother overheard her son, age four, tell his brother, age six, "I don't believe in Jesus." The brother responded, "You have really hurt my feelings." Sensing a need, the mother reinforced the younger boy's understanding of the Savior. She placed a picture of the Redeemer in his room and continued to teach all of her children more about the Master. Some time later, the younger son commented, "Mom, you're my best friend—next to Jesus."

Another mother has consistently read scriptures to her children to teach them truth. While overseas with no satisfactory schools, she spent much time and energy painstakingly tutoring them—with amazing results. Once the father went to help their five-year-old daughter with evening prayer. He found her kneeling, sharing her tender feelings with her Heavenly Father. Sensing his presence, she looked up. He said, "Do you know how wonderful it makes Father in Heaven feel when you talk to Him?" She responded, "Oh, Daddy, I will always talk to my Father in Heaven." Such is the pure heart of a five-year-old that has been carefully, spiritually nurtured.

Mothers like those have a vision of the power of obediently, patiently teaching truth, because they look beyond the peanut-butter sandwiches, soiled clothing, tedious hours of routine, struggles with homework, and long hours by a sickbed.

Let us be grateful to our Father in Heaven for His precious daughters. Let us help them as much as we can. Let us encourage every woman who questions her value to turn to her Heavenly Father and His glorified Son for a supernal confirmation of her immense individual worth. I testify that as each woman seeks that assurance in faith and obedience, the Savior will continually provide it through the Holy Ghost. That guidance will lead her to fulfillment, peace, and consuming joy through magnifying her divinely appointed, sacred womanhood.

Principle 14

A happy marriage results from making correct choices prayerfully together. It can transform a house into a place of heaven on earth.

OUR HEAVENLY FATHER endowed His sons and daughters with unique traits especially fitted for their individual responsibilities as they fulfill His plan. In the Lord's plan, it takes two—a man and a woman—to form a whole. Indeed, a husband and wife are not two identical halves, but a wondrous, divinely determined combination of complementary capacities and characteristics.

Marriage allows these different characteristics to come together in oneness—in unity—to bless a husband and wife, their children and grandchildren. For the greatest happiness and productivity in life, both husband and wife are needed. Their efforts interlock and are complementary. Each has individual traits that best fit the role the Lord has defined for happiness as a man or woman. When used as the Lord intends, those capacities allow a married couple to think, act, and rejoice as one—to face challenges together and overcome them as one, to grow in love and understanding, and through temple ordinances to be bound together as one whole, eternally. That is the plan.

With that in mind, I wish to discuss some things that you might do to bring oneness in your marriage. One is to recognize that spouses need each other. Marriage isn't a one-way street. The daughters of Father in Heaven are particularly giving. They are so giving that they don't know how good they are. Some men take that as a matter of course, as the way it is supposed to be: a husband being totally supported by his wife by the way she makes sacrifices. At night when the children are supposed to be asleep, for example, she gets up time and time again, when the husband hears that baby cry just as much as she does. Or maybe he works hard and comes home feeling he has had an exhausting day and needs to relax. She has probably had a more exhausting day, and he needs to be compensating in the way he supports her. I don't mean just physical help in the home, as important as that is. She needs to continue to develop her interests and her talents in appropriate ways. In order to do that, she needs time for it, and the husband can provide that time by the support he gives.

Some brethren don't recognize that there is a difference in how the priesthood is used in the home and how it is used in the Church. Because the Church is an organization where there are different levels, a hierarchical structure, we sometimes need to make decisions for those who are serving under us. In the home, the priesthood is not used that way. It is a patriarchal order. Who should make the decisions in the home?

The way of the Lord is that you make every decision together—period. And if you can't do that, you work until you do. You pray about it.

You will find the greatest happiness if you will base every decision on the question, "What does the Lord want us to do?" Seek together the will of the Lord. That, I believe, is the way to keep the balance we should.

Throughout your life on earth, seek diligently to fulfill the fundamental purposes of this life through the ideal family. While you may not have yet reached that ideal, do all you can through obedience and faith in the Lord to consistently draw as close to it as you are able. Don't become overanxious. Do the best you can. Living a pattern of life as close as possible to the ideal will provide much happiness, great satisfaction, and impressive growth here on earth.

Principle 15

The Spirit has taught me that Satan doesn't have to tempt us to do bad things—he can accomplish much of his objective by distracting us with many acceptable things, thus keeping us from accomplishing the essential ones.

ALTHOUGH OUR MEMORY of it is withheld, before we came to this earth we lived in the presence of God, our Eternal Father, and His Son, Jesus Christ. We shouted for joy when given the privilege of coming to this earth to receive a body and to move forward in God's plan for our happiness. We knew that we would be tested here. Part of that testing is to have so many seemingly interesting things to do that we can forget the main purposes for being here. Satan works very hard so that the essential things won't happen.

In quiet moments when you think about it, you recognize what is critically important in life and what isn't. Be wise and don't let good things crowd out those that are essential.

What are the essential ones? They are related to doctrine. They are centered in ordinances and embrace critical covenants. To receive all of the blessings of the Savior's atoning sacrifice, we are only asked to be obedient to His commandments and to receive *all* of the essential ordinances: baptism, confirmation, priesthood ordination for men, and temple ordinances. The Atonement will not only help us overcome our transgressions and mistakes, but, in His time, it will resolve all inequities of life—those things that are unfair which are the consequences of circumstance or others' acts and not our own decisions.

While some may not understand or agree, I testify that it is not sufficient to be baptized and then live an acceptable life, avoiding major transgressions. The Lord has decreed that the additional ordinances and covenants that I have mentioned must be received for exaltation and eternal life. Being worthy of temple ordinances means that you will choose to do what many in the world are not willing to do. You will keep the Sabbath day holy, exercise faith through the payment of tithing and fast offerings, consistently participate in Church worship, give service, and show love and appreciation for your family by helping each member of it. After you have received all of the temple ordinances, you will continue to grow by keeping the covenants made.

When obeyed, those covenants bring happiness and joy. They give purpose to life. Difficulty comes when agency is used to make choices that are inconsistent with those covenants. Study the things you do in your discretionary time, that time you are free to control. Do you find that it is centered in those things that are of highest priority and of greatest importance? Or do you unconsciously, consistently fill it with trivia and activities that are not of enduring value nor help you accomplish the purpose for which you came to earth? Think of the long view of life, not just what's going to happen today or tomorrow. *Don't give up what you most want in life for something you think you want now.*

Recognizing that you are a person who wants to live worthily and be obedient to Father in Heaven, how would Satan strive to lead you from the path to happiness? Surely he would not be successful by tempting you to commit serious transgression—at least not initially. He would more likely fill your mind and heart with visions of many, many worthwhile things—none of which could be criticized as being wrong, but, taken together, they would so occupy your time that you would not do those things that are absolutely essential for eternal life with Father in Heaven and His Beloved Son.

Find a retreat of peace and quiet where you can ponder and let the Lord establish the direction of your life. Each of us needs to check our bearings periodically and confirm that we are on course. Sometime soon you may benefit from taking this personal inventory:

• What are my highest priorities to be accomplished while on earth?

• How do I use my discretionary time? Is some of it consistently applied to my highest priorities?

• Is there anything I know I should not be doing? If so, I will repent and stop it now.

In a quiet moment, write down your responses. Analyze them. Make any necessary adjustments. Put first things first.

Why has your moral agency been given to you? Only to live a pleasurable life and to make choices to do the things you want to do? Or is there a more fundamental reason—to be able to make the choices that will lead you to fully implement your purpose for being here on earth? As you establish the correct priorities in your life, you will be assured of the development and happiness the Lord wants you to receive.

Principle 16

One of the most memorable and power-ful patterns of communication by the Spirit is through dreams. I have learned that when the transition from being fully asleep to being fully awake is almost imperceptible, it is a signal that the Lord has taught some-thing very important through a dream.

I N DREAMS, I HAVE on occasion been taught lessons that have changed my life. I would like to recount one such lesson.

When I awoke one night from a most disturbing dream, I ached physically, I was saturated with perspiration, and my heart was pounding. Every sense was sharpened. Although the actual dream was extensive, the key lessons communicated can be summarized by reference to a few specific experiences in the dream.

In it I found myself in a very different and unknown environment. Everything was strange to me. I could not recognize where I was or any of the individuals who surrounded me. I was anxiously seeking my wife, Jeanene. We had been separated, and I wanted very much to find her. Each individual I encountered said that I would not be able to do that. Repeatedly, as I sought in different directions to find her, I was emphatically told to forget her, for she would not be found. I was frustrated at every turn. One said, "She is no longer the same individual. There isn't a Jeanene like you knew."

I thought, "That is impossible. I know her, and I know she will never change."

Then I was told, "You are not the same. There is no individual by the name of Richard Scott, and soon all of the memories you've had of Jeanene, your children, and other loved ones will be eradicated."

Fear entered my heart, accompanied by a horrifying feeling. Then came the thought: "No, that is impossible. Those relationships are enduring and unchanging. As long as we live righteously, they cannot be eliminated. They are eternally fixed."

As more encounters came, I realized that I was surrounded with evil individuals who were completely unhappy, with no purpose save that of frustrating the happiness of others so that they too would become miserable. These wicked ones were striving to manipulate those persons over whom they sought to exercise control. I somehow was conscious that those who believed their lies were being led through treachery and deceit from what they wanted most. They soon began to believe that their individuality, their experience, and their relationships as families and friends were being altered and lost. They became angry, aggressive, and engulfed by feelings of hopelessness.

The pressure became more intense to accept as reality that what I had been no longer existed and that my cherished wife was no longer the same. I resisted those thoughts with every capacity that I could find. I was determined to find her. I knew that there must be a way and was resolute in searching no matter what the cost in time or effort.

It was then that I broke out of that oppressive surrounding and could see that it was an ugly, artificial, contrived environment. So intense were the feelings generated by what I had been told by those bent on destroying my hope to take me captive that I had not realized the forces of opposition that made my efforts appear fruitless could have no power over me unless I yielded through fear or abandonment of my principles. The environment appeared real, yet it had been generated from fear and threat. Although it was simulated, to those who let themselves believe the falsehoods thrust upon them it became reality.

I can now understand that because of my faith in the truths of the gospel plan, I could break through Satan's manipulative, evil environment to see it as it is—not only in the dream, but in real life as well—a confining, controlling, destructive influence that can be overcome by faith in and obedience to truth.

As I awoke, there flooded over me feelings of love and gratitude for our Heavenly Father and His Beloved Son that I do not have the capacity to express. My heart and mind filled with consuming love for Them and inexpressible appreciation for the blessings that are available to every spirit child of Father in Heaven willing to believe and be obedient to the plan of happiness. I cannot convey the unspeakable joy, the feeling of being wrapped in pure love, the absolute assurance that we will never lose our identity or memory of cherished relationships or the benefits of righteous acts as we continue to resist evil and are obedient to truth.

Although I would not welcome another like experience, this dream has taught me how easy it is to take for granted our relationship with our Father in Heaven and His Beloved Son, our Master and Savior. Oh, how blessed are we that They are as They say They are, perfect in every possible capacity and attribute.

Dreams are just one vehicle the Lord uses from time to time to convey a spiritual lesson. If you will remain aware, you can learn valuable truths from such experiences.

Principle 17

Sincere love has the potential to exercise power far beyond our limited understanding of love.

I AM CONVINCED THAT when we give unconditional love; when our interest is first in serving, building, edifying, strengthening without thought of self; when we do not expect an automatic return for each act of kindness, generosity, or sincere effort to help; when we are not concerned about what we will receive or what others will say or whether our own burdens will be diminished, but selflessly seek to build another, the miracle of the power of the gospel is released in our lives. When we permit the Lord to work through us to bless others, that sacred experience releases power in our own lives, and miracles occur. Well did the Master say, "For inasmuch as ye do it unto the least of these, ye do it unto me" (D&C 42:38). Respect and love must be earned, and there is no better way to earn them than to lift another. Begin now with your best effort. Reach out to another. You will feel the power of the Lord flow through you. Your own self-respect will return, and you can love yourself again. Your life will be enriched and given purpose, and you will be given the power to make a difference in everything around you.

Pure love is an incomparable, potent power for good. Righteous love is the foundation of a successful marriage. It is the primary cause of contented, well-developed children. It is the source of complete unity within a presidency, a quorum, or a family where decisions are voluntarily made unanimously. Where that unity comes willingly from a foundation of pure love and an eye single to the glory of God, vision, capacity and achievement are expanded by the power of God.

Love is a potent healer. Realizing that, Satan would separate you from the power of the love of God, kindred, and friends that want to help. He would lead you to feel that the walls are pressing in around you and there is no escape or relief. He wants you to believe you lack the capacity to help yourself and that no one else is really interested. If he succeeds, you will be driven to further despair and heartache. His strategy is to have you think you are not appreciated, loved, or wanted so that you in despair will turn to self-criticism, and in the extreme to even despising yourself and feeling evil when you are not. Remember the wisdom of the Lord "is greater than the cunning of the devil" (D&C 10:43). If you have such thoughts, break through those helpless feelings by reaching out in love to another in need. That may sound cruel and unfeeling when you long so much for healing, but it is based upon truth. Paul taught, "Bear ye one another's burdens, and so fulfil the law of Christ" (Galatians 6:2).

God has given you the capacity to exercise faith so that you may find peace, joy, and purpose in life. However, to employ its power, faith must be rooted in something secure. There is no more solid foundation than faith in the love Heavenly Father has for you, faith in His plan of happiness, and faith in the willingness and power of Jesus Christ to fulfill all of His promises.

Faith in Christ means you trust Him; you trust His teachings. That leads to hope, and hope brings charity, the pure love of Christ—that peaceful feeling that comes when you sense His concern, His love, and His capacity to cure you or to ease your burdens with His healing power.

Through His grueling, indescribably onerous sacrifice of self, Jesus Christ earned the authority and power to save us from the effect of broken law. He has done this through His matchless love and perfect Atonement. This act is the central ingredient of our Holy Father's plan of happiness. That is why the Atonement of Jesus Christ is considered to be the single most significant event that ever has or ever will occur.

I bear solemn witness that Jesus Christ lives. He is a glorious, manifestation of power and obedience. He is our Savior, our Redeemer, the Prince of Peace. He is all the hope that we have for eternal life with our Father in Heaven. I have found that He has the capacity to communicate love so intensely, so focused that it is beyond the capacity of the human tongue to describe adequately.

Principle 18

Satan's temptations are as a two-edged sword—we can be overcome by them or we can resist and gain strength until we can declare, "Get thee behind me, Satan."

S ATAN KNOWS THAT correct principles, when observed consistently, will render an individual increasingly resistant to his temptations. He has developed a comprehensive plan to undermine or destroy each one of them. For example, to dispose of faith, Satan would plant and cultivate in us the seeds of selfishness. He knows that if left unchecked, these seeds will grow into a monster that can enslave the divine spirit in man. Selfishness is at the root of sin. It leads to unrighteous acts that debauch and deprave the soul. It reinforces destructive habits that produce a dependence on chemical or physical stimulants that destroy the mind and body. Satan's program is based on immediate gratification of selfish desires. He urges us to participate now and pay later. However, the full, terrible consequences of payment are never revealed until it is tragically late. The Spirit of the Lord can overpower the stifling effect of selfishness. That cherished Spirit comes with faith, repentance, obedience, and service.

So that you will be forewarned, I will show you how Satan works. Let us imagine a boundary line, and assume that on one side of this boundary are all of the good things that can be done in life. They are arranged so that they get better and better as one moves farther from the boundary. On the other side are all the wrong things that can be done. They go from bad to worse. At the boundary it is difficult to discern what is right and what is wrong. That is where Satan tries to tempt righteous people. It is a twilight zone where you cannot clearly discern between what is good and what is bad, so it is easy to become confused. Live well within the area of good, and you won't have any problems with temptation.

I have never been sorry on any occasion when I stood for what was right—even against severe criticism. As you learn that truth, you will also discover that when you have taken a determined stand for right, when you have established personal standards and made covenants to keep them, when temptations come and you act according to your standards, you will be reinforced and given strength beyond your own capacity if that is needed. Difficulty comes when you enter the battle of temptation without a fixed plan. That is what Satan desires, for then you are ripe for defeat.

There is a vast difference between how Satan works and how the Lord works. If you understand these very simple things, you won't have any difficulty facing the challenges that come into your life.

Satan says there is no absolute truth. You make decisions on the basis of the circumstances. That pattern of rationalization—that is, taking something that is not true and twisting it so that it appears true—is his way to destroy you. The Lord says there is absolute truth. It is unchanging. You can count on it. You live your life on that foundation and you will not have any difficulty.

Satan says, "There is no God. No one is going to help you. Reach out and get all you can for yourself. That's the only way to really make it in this life." The Lord says, "Serve others. There is a God." I witness that He lives.

To those who make a mistake in life, especially a tragically important mistake, Satan says "Your life is through. You might as well continue; you've already ruined your life." The Lord says, "Through repentance, we can correct even the most serious transgressions." He has said, "He who has repented of his sins, the same is forgiven, and I, the Lord, remember them no more. By this ye may know if a man repenteth of his sins—behold, he will confess them and forsake them" (D&C 58:42–43).

Satan will attempt to reach you at your weakest point. Resist that temptation, and you will gain strength. Then he will try to tempt you at another point. Resist him, and you will gain strength, and he will become weaker. Then you can say, "Get thee behind me, Satan: for it is written, Thou shalt worship the Lord thy God, and him only shalt thou serve" (Luke 4:8).

What happens when we overcome challenges? We grow in strength. Now, that doesn't mean that we ought to go out and seek to be tempted. We ought to avoid temptation. But when we can't avoid it, we ought to overcome it. Let me give you some examples of what I mean.

In college I was given the privilege of joining a very elect honorary engineering society. As I attended the initiatory activities, everyone was drinking. I asked for a soft drink and was handed a glass. As I raised it to my lips, I could smell alcohol. I looked around the room. All the eyes were on me. These were professionals who had just given me a great honor. Should I pretend to drink so as not to offend? No. I sat the glass down and then noticed that three other inductees also sat their glasses aside. Do what is right and others will follow your example. Every time you make the right choice in the face of potential criticism, you build strength that makes it easier the next time. The reverse is also true. Satan counts on that.

One summer, as a teenager, I worked on an oyster boat off the coast of Long Island in New York to earn funds for college. The other members of the crew were seasoned oystermen, hardened by the harsh winter environment in which they spent much of their lives battling the icy ocean and raw wind to secure their catch. I was an enigma to them, easier to distrust than to understand. They shunned me as a company spy, then as a crazy kid who didn't know how to be a man. Later, I became better at my duties and tried to build friendships. They offered to make me a "real man" by joining them on their all-night indulgences. I thanked them but declined, and the tension grew more intense.

The summer weather was beautiful and the ocean magnificent. We were engaged in relatively simple tasks, such as transferring small oysters to a more distant portion of the sound where the nutrients accelerated their growth and improved their flavor. Except when a dredge full of oysters was dumped onto the deck, signaling a flurry of intense activity, there was much time for contemplation. While my deck mates dozed by their shovels, I read and pondered the content of the Book of Mormon. I cannot adequately express the powerful awakening within me that came from those weeks of study of the Book of Mormon under singularly unusual circumstances.

We slept in envelope-type bunks sandwiched into the restricted space between the ship's diesel engine and hull. One night at dockside I retired early since some of the crew planned unrighteous activity outside our boat. I was suddenly shaken into consciousness by the powerful hand of a deck mate, Toddy, a giant of a man. He was brandishing a hammer in my face, and his breath reeked of alcohol. Stunned, I realized that there was no way that I could escape him. I thought I had come to the end of the road. Then I heard what he was shouting, "Scotty, get your fins and mask. There's a man overboard, and you can save him."

That night I learned a lesson I have never forgotten. Publicly the crew members ridiculed me, but privately they respected me for my standards. The confidence that came from that knowledge let me quietly help three of them with some serious personal challenges.

A decisive, correct choice made once and consistently kept thereafter will avoid much heartache. You then can use your energy in keeping your resolve rather than repeatedly wrestling with the same challenge. Also, you will greatly reduce the possibility that you will be overcome by temptation.

Principle 19

In a quiet moment of pondering, I learned that there is a relationship between faith and character. The greater our faith in Jesus Christ, the stronger our character, and increased character enhances our ability to exercise even greater faith.

WHEN FAITH IS PROPERLY understood and used, it has dramatically far-reaching effects. Such faith can transform an individual's life from maudlin, common, everyday activities to a symphony of joy and happiness. The exercise of faith is vital to Father in Heaven's plan of happiness.

Faith is a foundation building block of creation. I am confident that the Savior Jesus Christ uses faith in His capacity to act under the direction of Father in Heaven. The Master used it to create the most remote galaxies as well as to compose quarks, the smallest elements of matter we know of today.

Faith and character are intimately related. Faith in the power of obedience to the commandments of God will forge strength of character available to you in times of urgent need. Such character is not developed in moments of great challenge or temptation. That is when it is intended to be used. Your exercise of faith in true principles builds character; fortified character expands your capacity to exercise more faith. As a result, your capacity and confidence to conquer the trials of life is enhanced.

We *become* what we want to *be* by consistently *being* what we want to *become* each day. Righteous character is a precious manifestation of what you are becoming. Righteous character is more valuable than any material object you own, any knowledge you have gained through study, or any goals you have attained no matter how well lauded by mankind. In the next life your righteous character will be evaluated to assess how well you used the privilege of mortality.

Strong moral character results from consistent correct choices in the trials and testing of life. Such choices are made with trust in things that are believed and when acted upon are confirmed. Faith is an important element in developing that trust.

What are some of the empowering principles upon which faith is based?

• Trust in God and in His willingness to provide help when needed, no matter how challenging the circumstance.

• Obedience to His commandments and a life that demonstrates that He can trust you.

• Sensitivity to the quiet promptings of the Holy Spirit.

• Courageous implementation of that prompting.

• Patience and understanding when God lets you struggle to grow and when answers come a piece at a time.

Every time you try your faith—that is, act in worthiness on an impression—you will receive the confirming evidence of the Spirit. As you walk to the boundary of your understanding into the twilight of uncertainty, exercising faith, you will be led to find solutions you would not obtain otherwise.

With even your strongest faith, God will not always reward you immediately according to your desires. Rather, God will respond with what in His eternal plan is best for you, when it will yield the greatest advantage. Be thankful that sometimes God lets you struggle for a long time before that answer comes. That causes your faith to increase and your character to grow.

The bedrock of character is integrity. Worthy character will strengthen your capacity to recognize the direction of the Spirit and to be obedient to it. A secure foundation for your growing character is laid by making Jesus Christ and His teachings the center of your life.

Your happiness on earth as well as your eternal salvation require many correct decisions, none of which is too difficult to make. Together those decisions with the help of the Lord forge a character resistant to the eroding influences of sin and transgression. Noble character is like a treasured porcelain made of select raw materials, formed with faith, carefully crafted by consistent righteous acts, and fired in the furnace of challenging experience. It is an object of great beauty and priceless worth. Yet it can be damaged in a moment through transgression, requiring painful, prolonged effort to be rebuilt. When protected by self-control, righteous character will endure for eternity.

Material things do not of themselves produce happiness and satisfaction and the joy of attainment on earth. Nor do they lead us to exaltation. It is nobility of character, that fabric of inner strength and conviction woven from countless righteous decisions, that gives life its direction. A consistent, righteous life produces an inner power and strength that can be permanently resistant to the destructive influence of sin and transgression. Your faith in Jesus Christ and obedience to His commandments will strengthen your character. Your character is a measure of what you are becoming. It is the evidence of how well you are using your time on earth in this period of mortal probation.

Principle 20

Forced obedience yields no enduring fruit. That is why both our Father in Heaven and the Savior are willing to entreat, to prompt, to encourage, and to patiently wait for us to recognize precious spiritual guidance from Them.

I HAVE COME TO KNOW that there are currents of divine influence in our life that will lead each of us along the individual plan the Lord would have us follow while on earth. They are identified through the whisperings of the Holy Spirit. Seek through that Spirit to identify that plan and carefully follow the direction the Lord will provide. It will come through answers to prayers and pondering or the counsel of others who are worthy mentors. Align yourself with it. Choose, willingly, to exercise your agency to follow it. Do not be overcome by concentrating solely on today, its challenges, difficulties, and opportunities. Those things are the relatively insignificant surface winds and waves of today. Such preoccupations must not totally capture your interest and attention so as to consume your life.

The more closely you follow the current of divine guidance, the greater will be your happiness here and for eternity. Moreover, your capacity to progress and serve will be greater. I do not understand entirely how it is done, but this divine current does not take away your moral agency. However, I do know that as you seek to know the will of the Lord in your life, you will more easily discern that divine current. The right of moral agency is so important to our Father in Heaven that He was willing to lose one-third of His spirit children so that it would be preserved. No enduring improvement can occur without righteous exercise of agency.

The Lord will not force you to learn. You must exercise your agency to authorize the Spirit to teach you. As you make this a practice in your life, you will be more perceptive to the feelings that come with spiritual guidance. Then, when that guidance comes, sometimes when you least expect it, you will recognize it more easily.

Who does not have need of assurance in times of uncertainty and testing? Who is so self-confident that there is never want for a stabilizing influence in life? A fundamental purpose of earth life is personal growth and attainment. Consequently, there must be times of trial and quandary to provide opportunity for that development. What child could ever grow to be self-supporting in maturity if all the critical decisions were made by parents? So it is with our Heavenly Father. He will never override our agency by forcing us to obey. His plan of happiness is conceived so that we will have challenges, even difficulties, where decisions of great importance must be made so that we can grow, develop, and succeed in this mortal probation. Gratefully, in His perfect love, He has provided a way for us to resolve those challenges while growing in strength and capacity. I speak of the sustaining power of faith in times of uncertainty and testing.

God has given us the capacity to exercise faith, that we may find peace, joy, and purpose in life. However, for some, faith is not understood and consequently not used to full advantage. Some feel that any discussion of religion and the guidance one can receive through robust faith have no rational basis. However, faith is not an illusion or magic but a power rooted in eternal principles. Are you one who has tried to exercise faith and has felt no benefit? If so, you likely have not understood and followed the principles upon which faith is founded. An example will illustrate what I mean.

Years ago I participated in the measurement of the nuclear characteristics of different materials. The process used an experimental nuclear reactor designed so that high energy particles streamed from a hole in the center of the reactor. These particles were directed into an experimental chamber where measurements were made. The high-energy particles could not be seen, but they had to be carefully controlled to avoid harm to others. One day a janitor entered while we were experimenting. In a spirit of disgust he said, "You are all liars, pretending that you are doing something important, but you can't fool me. I know that if you can't see, hear, taste, smell, or touch it, it doesn't exist." That attitude ruled out the possibility of his learning that there is much of worth that can't be identified by the five senses. Had that man been willing to open his mind to understand how the presence of nuclear particles is detected, he would have confirmed their existence. In like manner, never doubt the reality of faith.

The axiom "You get what you pay for" is true for spiritual rewards as well as temporal concerns. You get what you pay for in obedience, in faith in Jesus Christ, in diligent application of the truths that you learn. What you get is the molding of your character, with growth in capacity, and the successful completion of your purpose here on earth, which is to grow through being proven.

Principle 21

It is important not to judge ourselves by what we think we know of our own potential. We should trust the Lord and what He can do with our dedicated heart and willing mind (see D&C 64:34).

MOST OF US THINK we know our own limits, but much of what we "know" isn't knowledge at all, but belief: erroneous, self-limiting belief. When we live righteously, study conscientiously, striving to do what is right because we want to, because it is our personal choice to do so, we release the power of the Lord in our lives. This exercise of moral agency permits inspiration to flow into our minds and hearts, and we are strengthened and supported from on high. As members of the Church, we have the gift of the Holy Ghost, which can give us a tremendous assist over others of equivalent background and native capacity.

Recently I watched more than 20,000 young Latter-day Saint men and women listen to a spiritual message. They took notes and concentrated on the speaker, anxious to learn. There radiated from them an intense spirit of purity, righteousness, and devotion. No one had forced them to come. They wanted to be there.

Later I met with more than 2,000 full-time missionaries preparing to serve. The room was charged with the Spirit. I asked them difficult questions. They responded extremely well, often citing supporting scriptures. As I shook missionaries' hands and looked into their eyes, I felt purity and a spirit of devotion. It was an inspiring experience. Each had set aside personal interests to accept a call to join what can become our greatest generation of missionaries.

I have had like experiences with youth across the earth. The faculty at the Church universities note a significant increase in capacity and spiritual sensitivity of students. Something extra-ordinary is happening. Do you sense it? Truly, as obedience and morality decline in the world, the Lord is sending more excep-tional spirits to earth. As a group they excel the average capacity of their forebears. Their potential for personal growth and posi-tive contribution is enormous. As parents and leaders, how are you cultivating that potential? As a young man or woman of this generation, what are you doing to realize your extraordinary po-tential? Will you nurture it and rise to exceptional heights of ac-complishment and happiness? How will you avoid Satan's efforts to undermine your potential through transgression? Only you can answer these critical questions.

With all my capacity I encourage you to discover who you really are. I invite you to look beyond the daily routine of life. I urge you to discern through the Spirit your divinely given capac-ities. I exhort you to prayerfully make worthy choices that will lead you to realize your full potential. When you push against the boundaries of experience into the twilight of the unknown, the Lord will strengthen you. The beauty of your eternal soul will begin to unfold.

High performers focus more intently on bettering their own previous efforts than on beating competitors. Compete with yourself, not others. I am not necessarily saying to work harder. To improve may simply mean to work more intelligently.

Study the First Vision as recorded in Joseph Smith—History

in the Pearl of Great Price. Learn of the subsequent events that brought the full restoration of truth, with the priesthood authority and ordinances essential to exaltation. Gain your own testimony of these things. Fix them in your mind and heart.

Try reading the Book of Mormon because you want to, not because you have to. Discover for yourself that it is true. As you read each page ask, "Could any man have written this book or did it come as Joseph Smith testified?" Apply the teachings you learn. They will fortify you against the evil of Satan. Follow Moroni's counsel. Sincerely ask God the Father, in the name of Jesus Christ, with real intent, if the teachings of the Book of Mormon are true (see Moroni 10:3–5). Ask with a desire to receive a confirmation personally, nothing doubting. There has to be an explanation of that book you can hold in your hand. I know that you can receive a spiritual confirmation that it is true. You will then know that Jesus Christ lives, that Joseph Smith was and is a prophet, and that The Church of Jesus Christ of Latter-day Saints is the Lord's Church (see introduction to the Book of Mormon, especially the last paragraph). You will confirm that the Savior guides His Church through a living prophet. These truths will become a secure foundation for your productive life.

One may say, "I don't have all the blessings of an ideal family and full Church experience." Neither did I enjoy all of those advantages, nor did some other members of the Quorum of the Twelve. Compensate by obtaining your own unwavering testimony of truth. Obtain a personal conviction that the Church of Jesus Christ has been restored to earth and that His doctrines are true. There are different paths to that treasured gift. They begin with your sincere desire to know. The flickering flame of faith can die if you do not nurture it. But that tiny flame can grow into a brilliant, unquenchable fire through sincere prayer and consistent study of the Book of Mormon and other scriptures. Such faith will be sustained as you apply the principles you learn.

Remain worthy. When you really understand who you are, it is not difficult to resist Satan's temptations. Then he can't thwart the development of your true potential.

Your goals may be noble, but you decide by the choices you make each day whether they will be realized or not. A knowledge of truth is of little value unless lived in full measure.

The foundation of happiness is to work hard and to obey willingly the principles of truth, confident that the Lord will open doors of help when needed. Our Father in Heaven will not violate His plan. He will not give eternal blessings to those who want them but have not paid the price in repentance (when needed) and consistent obedience. All of the richest blessings Father in Heaven has in store are within the reach of every individual who submits to the will of the Father and consistently lives His commandments and receives all of the ordinances and covenants he or she is able to have in this life.

If you think it is too hard, that you are imperfect and will not be able to do it, you are slipping into Satan's world. Garner strength by remembering that you can do anything the Lord asks you to do. When needed, He will see that you get the required help as you do all you are capable of doing. It is the intent of our Father in Heaven to take you from your current state of progression to the highest levels of attainment in celestial worlds. You don't know how He can do it, yet by meeting each test you demonstrate your faith in the Savior and in the plan of your holy Father. Though you do not see the end from the beginning, your trust in Them will give you the capacity to overcome.

Conclusion

I testify that as you are prayerful and seek the guidance of the Spirit, you can identify over a period of time important things the Lord wants you to accomplish. I say that with absolute conviction of its truth. I have lived that principle; you can live it. Don't make mistakes of judgment along the way that lead you to transgress the laws of God. There is no happiness there. There is no success there. Be resolute in your determination. Be clean and pure and worthy of the companionship of the Holy Ghost. I know that as you exercise faith, no matter what happens in the world, you will be successful and happy. There may be some challenging growth experiences and some sadness, but your life will be crowned with success and joy.

I bear witness that Jesus Christ knows you personally. He will provide answers to every difficult problem in your life as you trust Him and do all that you can to understand and apply His doctrine and strive to live by the Spirit.